Buddha Doodles
Gratitude Journal

Shining Your Light

by Molly Hahn (Mollycules)

Published by Buddha Doodles
Copyright Molly Hahn
ISBN-13: 978-0615905211
Nov 2013

How to use this journal:

- keep this near your bed or favorite place to sit

- write the date

- write 3 or more things you're grateful for

- repeat daily :)

Forever is now.

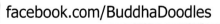

"There is nothing stronger in
the world than gentleness."

— Han Suyin

Learn to love what you normally resist.

" A little nonsense
now and then
is cherished by
the wisest men. "

~ Roald Dahl

DATE:

You are precious.

Share what you love!

DATE:

" You are the universe,

expressing itself as human.

for a little while." ~Eckhart Tolle

"Realizations are like shooting stars."
~Adyashanti

DATE:

"It is up to us to keep
the wheel turning for the
happiness of others."
~ Thich Nhat Hanh

Create

gift

inspire!

"Joy is being together,
not what one does."
~Tonia Shimin

Grace is ever-present.

Direct the mind
to the present moment.

_____   _____
_____   _____
_____   _____
_____   _____
_____   _____
_____   _____

_____
_____

                            _____
                            _____
                            _____
                            _____
                            _____
                            _____

Every moment is an
opportunity for meditation.

DATE:

Our breath is the key to coming back to THIS MOMENT.

Invite your SouL
to come out
and PLAY!

_____   _____

_____   _____

_____   _____

_____   _____

_____   _____

"Embrace your suffering,
and let it reveal to you
the way to peace."
~Thich Nhat Hanh

_____

_____

_____

_____

_____

_____

_____

_____

_____   _____

_____   _____

_____   _____

_____   _____

" Be happy in the moment, that's enough. Each moment is all we need, not more. "

~ Mother Teresa

"Everyday find ways to make your LOVE evident in the world."

~Zhena Muzyka

DATE:

"Happy teachers will change the world."
-Thich Nhat Hanh

Blessed are we.

_____ _____
_____ _____
_____ _____
_____ _____
_____ _____

" It always seems
impossible
until it's
done. "

~Nelson
Mandela

_____

_____

_____

_____

_____

" Health is the greatest possession.
Contentment is the greatest treasure.
Non-being is the greatest joy."
~Lao Tzu

DATE:

_____   _____

_____   _____

_____   _____

_____   _____

_____   _____

"Remembering a wrong is like carrying
a burden on the mind." — Buddha

_____

_____

_____

_____

_____   _____
_____   _____
_____   _____
_____   _____

"Drink your tea slowly and reverently,
as if it is the axis on which the earth
revolves—slowly, evenly, without rushing
toward the future."

                              —Thich Nhat Hanh

_____

_____

_____

_____

_____   _____

_____   _____

_____   _____

_____   _____

_____   _____

~ Ask your heart ~
~ Rest in stillness ~
~ Allow the answer to arise ~

_____

_____

_____

_____

_____

Keep it light.

_____

_____

_____

_____

_____   _____

_____   _____

_____   _____

_____   _____

_____   _____

_____   _____

_____   _____

_____   _____

_____   _____

_____   _____

Be the mantra.

_____

_____

_____

_____

_____

DATE:

_____   _____
_____   _____
_____   _____
_____   _____
_____   _____

Dare to DREAM.

_____
_____
_____
_____
_____

_____   _____
_____   _____
_____   _____
_____   _____
_____   _____

Observe your storylines

with compassion.

_____
_____
_____
_____

_____   _____

_____   _____

_____   _____

_____   _____

_____   _____

It's okay to rest.

_____

_____

_____

_____

_____

_____

_____

_____

_____

_____

_____

"Love more, fear less.
Float more, steer less."

-John 'Halcyon' Styn

_____

_____

_____

_____

_____

_____

_____   _____
_____   _____
_____   _____
_____   _____
_____   _____

$$f(x) = \sqrt{i}$$

$$e = mc^2$$

"I did not come to my fundamental understanding of the universe through my rational mind."

—Albert Einstein

_____

_____

_____

_____

_____

DATE:

_____

_____

_____

_____

_____

_____

_____

Stay Strong
and

_____

_____

_____

_____

_____

_____

Sparkle On!

" From wonder into wonder,
        existence opens. "
            ～Lao Tzu

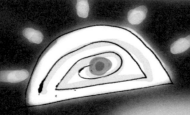

" The quieter
you become,
the more that
you
can hear."

~Ram Dass

.Be still.

_____ _____

_____ _____

_____ _____

_____ _____

_____ _____

"New beginnings are often disguised as painful endings."
~Lao Tzu

_____

_____

_____

_____

_____

_____

_____

_____

_____

_____

_____   _____

_____   _____

_____   _____

_____   _____

_____   _____

OPEN.

Allow the
waves of BEING
to wash through
you.

Stay curious.

DATE:

Surrender your worries
to the sea.

DATE:

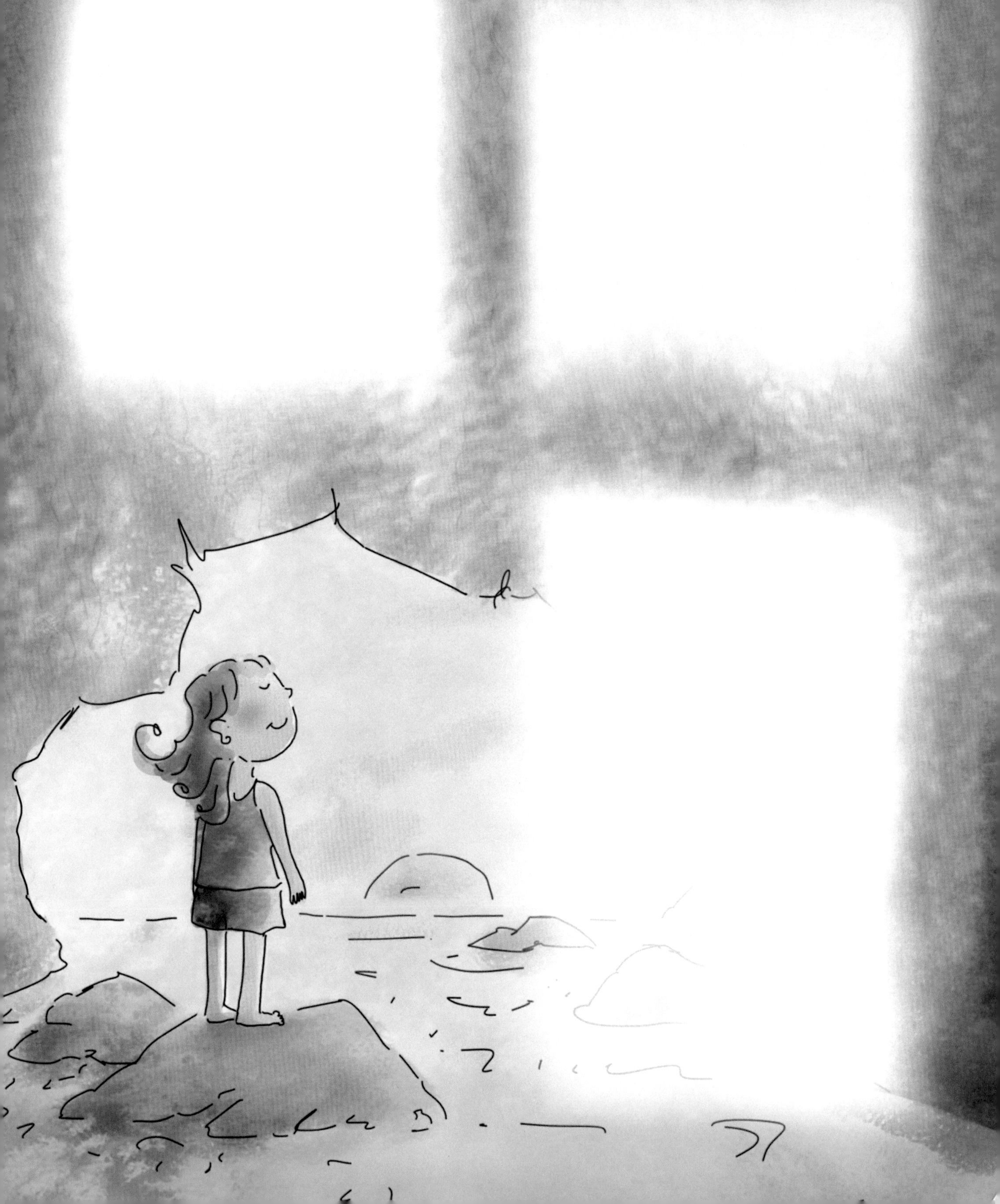

_____   _____

_____   _____

_____   _____

_____   _____

_____   _____

Cultivate joy.

_____

_____

_____

_____

_____

DATE:

_____

_____

_____

_____

_____

_____

_____

_____

_____

_____

_____

_____

_____

_____

" The truth is already
in you. "
~ Thich Nhat Hanh

_____   _____

_____   _____

_____   _____

_____   _____

_____   _____

Breathe love into your heart's wounds. Let that become the object of your meditation.

_____

_____

_____

_____

Incline your mind towards kindness.

_____   _____
_____   _____
_____   _____
_____   _____
_____   _____

Rest in the space that
nourishes your Soul.

_____
_____
_____
_____
_____

_____   _____
_____   _____
_____   _____
_____   _____
_____   _____

"The boat I can feel
So lonely in actually holds us all."

—Mary Karr

_____
_____
_____
_____
_____

Love will propel
you anywhere.

DATE:

Swing as HIGH as you CAN
on a SWINGSET, by Moonlight.
~SARK

_____   _____

_____   _____

_____   _____

_____   _____

_____   _____

Give yourself permission
to break routine.

_____

_____

_____

_____

_____

DATE:

_____   _____

_____   _____

_____   _____

_____   _____

_____   _____

"Be here now."
~Ram Dass

_____

_____

_____

_____

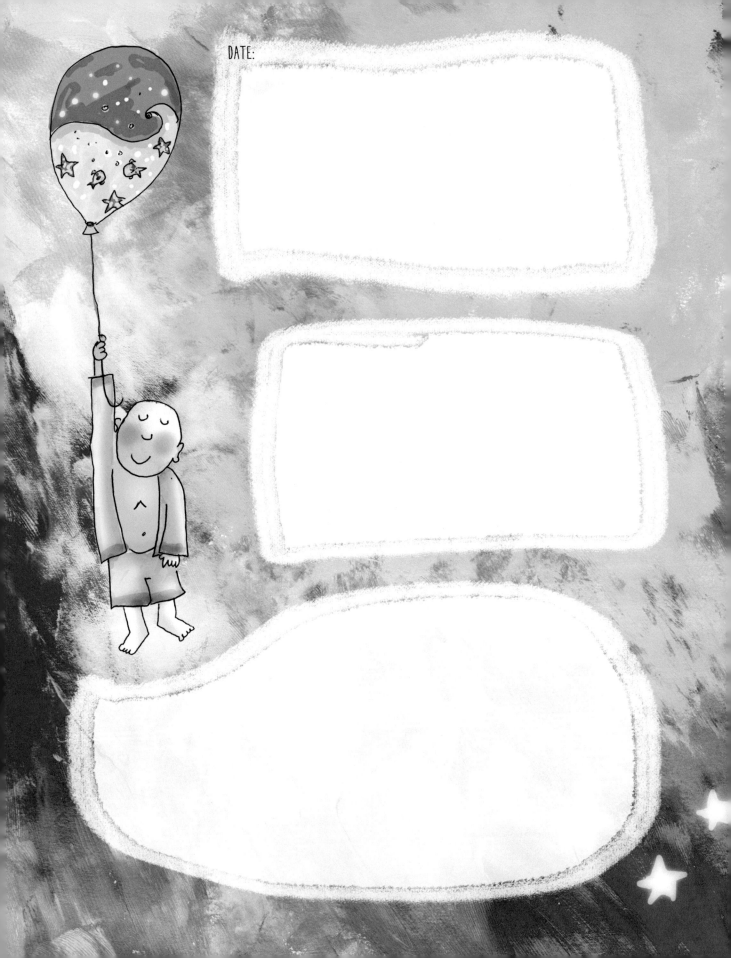

DATE:

"Absolute
attention
is prayer."
~ Zen Saying

_____   _____
_____   _____
_____   _____
_____   _____
_____   _____

Compassion for self, compassion for others.

_____

_____

_____

_____

_____   _____

_____   _____

_____   _____

_____   _____

_____   _____

Make watering your seeds
of happiness a daily practice.

_____

_____

_____

_____

"In its true state consciousness is naked, immaculate, clear, vacuous, transparent, timeless, beyond all conditions.

O Nobly Born, remember the pure open sky of your own true nature."

~ Tibetan Book of Great Liberation

DATE:

DATE:

Through darkness,
we find light.

DATE:

Fill perceptions of
lack with LOVE!

_____   _____

_____   _____

_____   _____

_____   _____

_____   _____

Find stillness in movement.

_____

_____

_____

_____

_____

DATE:

_____

_____

_____

_____

" Peace begins with
a smile. "
~Mother Teresa

_____

_____

_____

_____

_____

_____

_____

_____

_____

_____   _____

_____   _____

_____   _____

_____   _____

_____   _____

Honor your goodness
and the
goodness of others.

_____

_____

_____

_____

_____

Be love.

" What you seek
is seeking you."
~Rumi

_____   _____

_____   _____

_____   _____

_____   _____

_____   _____

Bless a stranger.

_____

_____

_____

_____

_____

_____

_____

_____

_____

" When you've touched
one person's heart,
you've changed
the whole world
forever. "

~Rebekah Borucki
#BLISSEDIN

_____

_____

_____

_____

_____

_____

_____

DATE:

Cultivate contentment.

Love and compassion for all beings.

DATE:

The freedom of heart is LOVE.

DATE:

Every part of you
is sacred.

Make space to listen
to your wise
        heart.
What you seek
        lies within.

_____

_____

_____

_____

_____

_____

_____

_____

_____

_____

_____

_____

_____

"Mindfulness is the energy that brings the eyes of Buddha into our hand." — Thich Nhat Hanh

_____

_____

_____

_____

_____

Listen with your whole being.

_____   _____

_____   _____

_____   _____

_____   _____

      ---

yogas citta vrtti nirodhah   yogas citta vrtti nirodhah

Observe the fluctuations of the mind.

"What would You have me do?
Where would You have me go?
What would You have me say, and
to whom?"
˄ A Course in Miracles

_____

_____

_____

_____

_____   _____

_____   _____

_____   _____

_____   _____

_____ _____

_____ _____

_____ _____

_____ _____

_____ _____

"The courageous heart is
the one that is unafraid to open
itself to the world."

~Jack Kornfield

_____

_____

_____

_____

DATE:

_____

_____

_____

_____

_____

_____

_____

_____

_____

_____

_____

_____

_____

_____

LIVE COLORFULLY!

_____

_____

_____

_____

_____

Our love
is our
wisdom.

Our wisdom
is our
love.

_____   _____

_____   _____

_____   _____

_____   _____

"To the mind that is
still, the whole
universe surrenders."

~Lao Tzu

DATE:

" Tonight the moon
kisses the stars. "
~Rumi

_____

_____

_____

_____

_____

_____

_____

_____

_____

_____

_____

"We're our own dragons
as well as our
own heroes, and we have
to rescue ourselves
from ourselves."

— TOM ROBBINS

_____   _____

_____   _____

_____   _____

_____   _____

_____   _____

_____

_____

_____

_____

_____   _____

_____   _____

_____   _____

_____   _____

_____

"Your vision will become clear only when you look into your heart. Who looks outside, dreams. Who looks inside, awakens." ~Carl Jung

_____

_____

_____

_____

_____   _____
_____   _____
_____   _____
_____   _____
_____   _____

" Compassion is our deepest
nature. It arises from our interconnection
with all things."

~Jack Kornfield

_____
_____
_____
_____

_____   _____

_____   _____

_____   _____

_____   _____

_____   _____

_____   _____

_____   _____

_____   _____

_____   _____

"As we let our own light
shine, we unconsciously give
others permission to
do the same."
~Marianne
        Williamson

"Don't be pushed by your problems. Be led by your dreams."
~Ralph Waldo Emerson

_____   _____

_____   _____

_____   _____

_____   _____

_____   _____

Your inbox will never be
completely empty.

_____

_____

_____

_____

♥Dance like nobody's watching♥

_____

_____

_____

_____

_____

_____

_____

"Be faithful in small things because it is in them that your strength lies."

—Mother Teresa

_____

_____

_____

_____

_____

_____

_____

_____

_____
_____
_____
_____
_____
_____

"Love yourself out loud!"

~Rebekah Borucki
#BLISSEDIN

_____
_____
_____
_____

_____
_____
_____
_____
_____
_____

_____   _____
_____   _____
_____   _____
_____   _____
_____   _____

If nothing else, be kind.

_____
_____
_____
_____

_____   _____
_____   _____
_____   _____
_____   _____
_____   _____

" All the elements for your happiness
are already here. There is no need to
run, strive, search, or struggle.
Just be. "

~ Thich Nhat Hanh

_____
_____
_____
_____

"Everything in the universe is
within you. Ask all from yourself."
~ Rumi

" Radiate boundless love
towards the entire world — above, below,
and across — unhindered, without
ill will, without enmity. " ~Buddha

This too shall pass.

Made in the USA
Middletown, DE
09 July 2018